How to Cursive

HANDWRITING PRACTICE WORKBOOK

By Goldstar Workbooks

Copyright © 2018 DGT Book Promotions, LLC
Published by DGT Book Promotions, LLC
All rights reserved.
Cover art obtained from Pixabay.com
ISBN-13: 978-1986843300
ISBN-10: 1986843300

LEARN HOW TO WRITE IN CURSIVE!

CURSIVE IS A STYLE OF PENMANSHIP IN WHICH THE LETTERS ARE JOINED TOGETHER IN A FLOWING AND LOOPING MANNER FOR THE PURPOSE OF MAKING WRITING FASTER. ALTHOUGH MANY SCHOOLS IN THE UNITED STATES NO LONGER TEACH CURSIVE HANDRWRITING HISTORICAL DOCUMENTS SUCH AS THE UNITED STATES CONSTITUTION ARE WRITTEN IN CURSIVE AND DOCUMENTS STILL REQUIRE A SIGNATURE WHICH IS GENERALLY CONSIDERED TO BE WRITTEN IN CURSIVE. TEACH YOUR CHILD THE TIME TREASURED SKILL OF HOW TO READ AND WRITE CURSIVE THROUGH THE PRACTICE PAGES IN THIS BOOK.

WHAT'S INSIDE:

- LARGE 8 X 10 INCH PAGES AND A CURSIVE LETTER REFERENCE CHART
- TWO PAGES OF UPPER AND LOWER CASE PRACTICE PAGES FOR EACH LETTER
- SENTENCES TO PRACTICE CONNECTING CURSIVE LETTERS
- DOTTED LETTERS, NUMBERS, ARROWS AND A STARTING POINT DOT TO HELP GUIDE THE DIRECTION TO WRITE THE LETTERS
- BLANK LINES ON EACH PAGE TO PRACTICE WRITING ON YOUR OWN
- A LIST OF LINKS TO FREE ONLINE VIDEOS AND APPS TO HELP YOU LEARN HOW TO FORM CURSIVE LETTERS

Aa Bb Cc

Dd Ee Ff

Gg Hh Ii

Jj Kk Ll

Mm Nn Oo

Pp Qq Rr

Ss Tt Uu

Vv Ww Xx

Yy Zz

Upper and Lower Case Letter A

Upper and Lower Case Letter A

Connect the letters and write the sentences

She eats an apple.

She eats an apple.

She eats an apple.

Upper and Lower Case Letter B

Upper and Lower Case Letter B

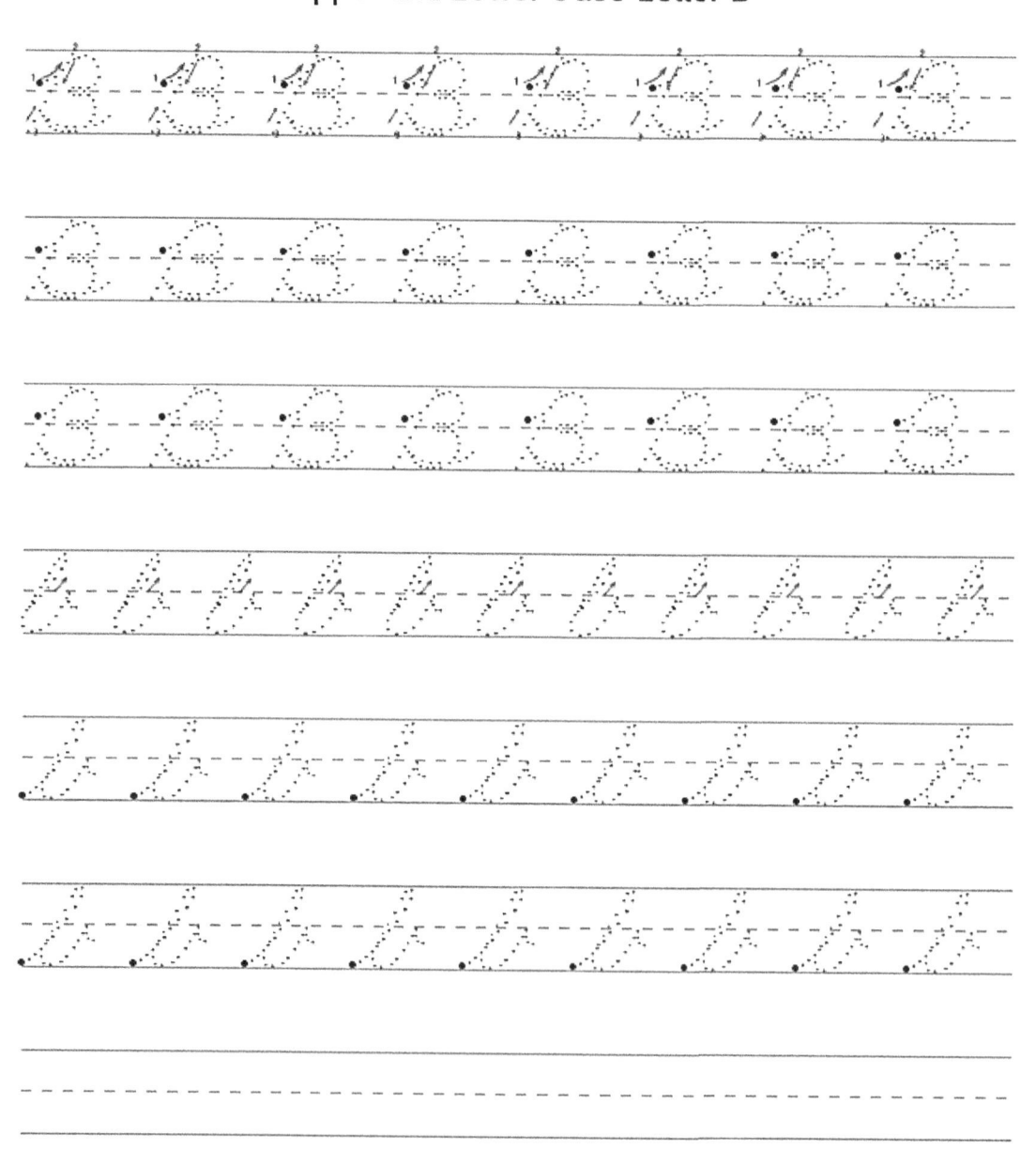

Connect the letters and write the sentences

Betty bit a banana.

Betty bit a banana.

Betty bit a banana.

Upper and Lower Case Letter C

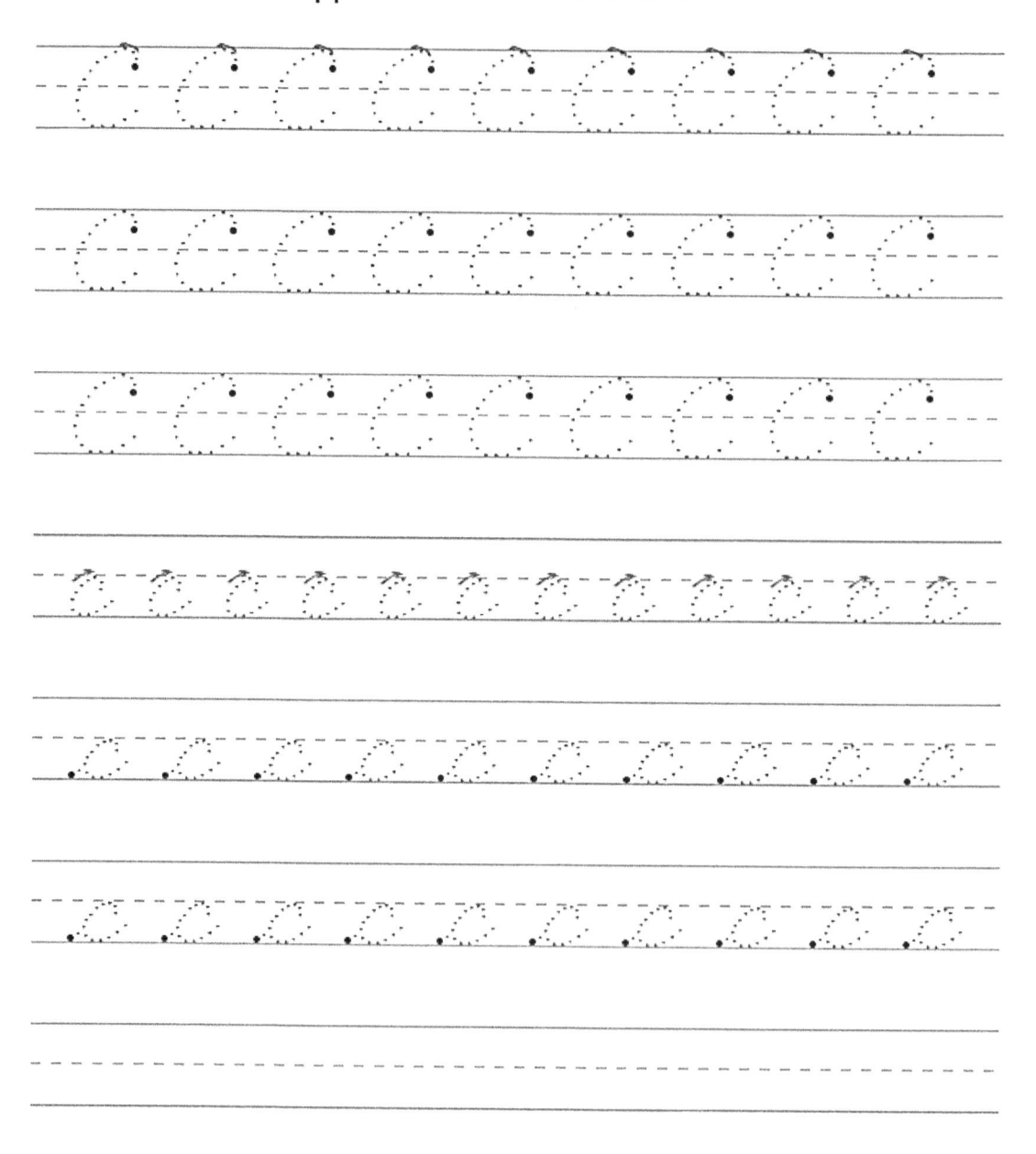

Connect the letters and write the sentences

Cathy cuts a carrot.

Cathy cuts a carrot.

Cathy cuts a carrot.

Upper and Lower Case Letter D

Upper and Lower Case Letter D

Connect the letters and write the sentences

Every dog has dinner.

I'm a dog as

dinner.

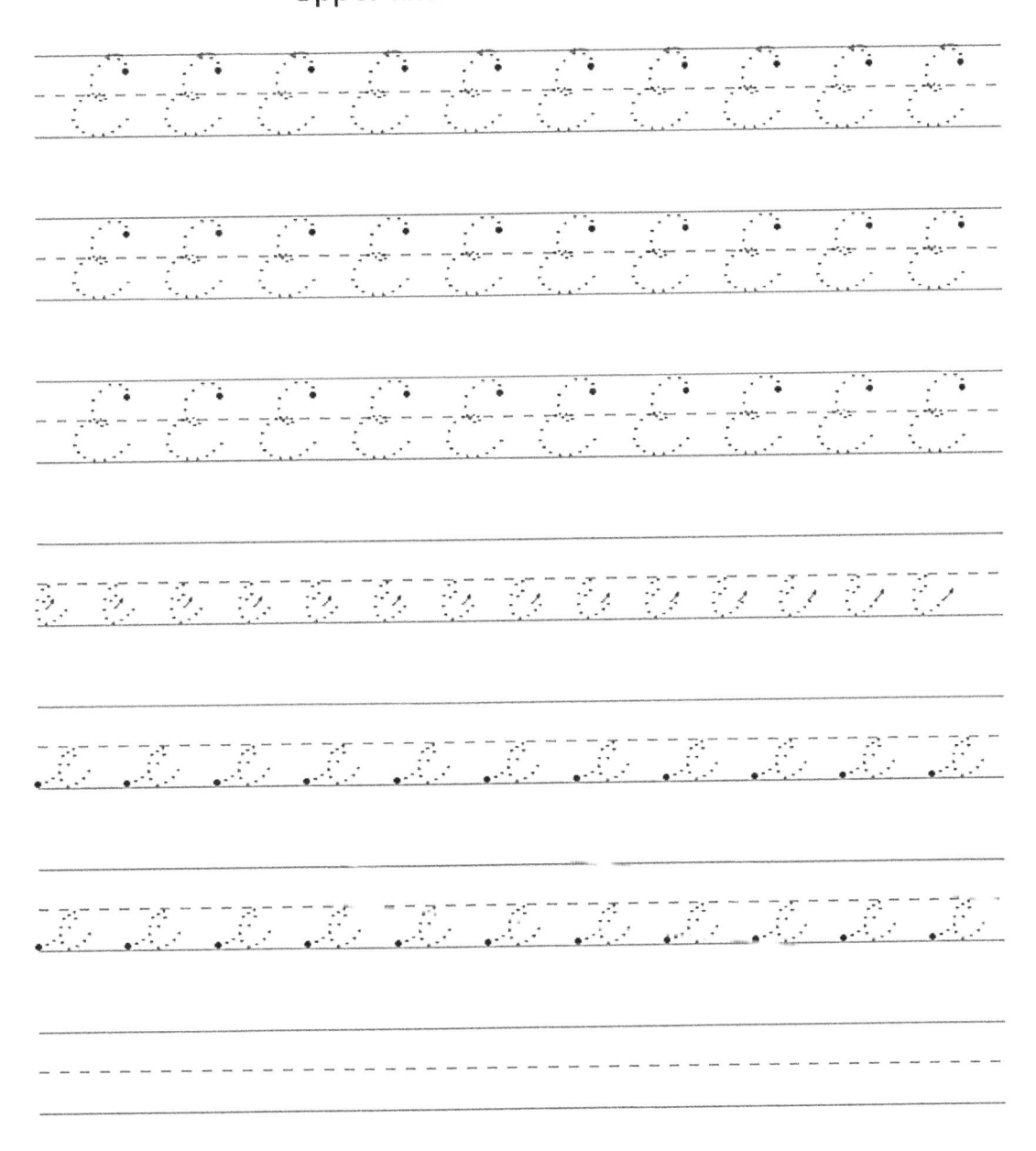

Upper and Lower Case Letter E

Upper and Lower Case Letter E

Connect the letters and write the sentences

Upper and Lower Case Letter F

Upper and Lower Case Letter F

Connect the letters and write the sentences

Frank finds a fawn.

Frank finds a fawn.

Frank finds a fawn.

Upper and Lower Case Letter G

Upper and Lower Case Letter G

Connect the letters and write the sentences

I hope you are fine.

I hope you are fine.

I hope you are fine.

Upper and Lower Case Letter H

Upper and Lower Case Letter H

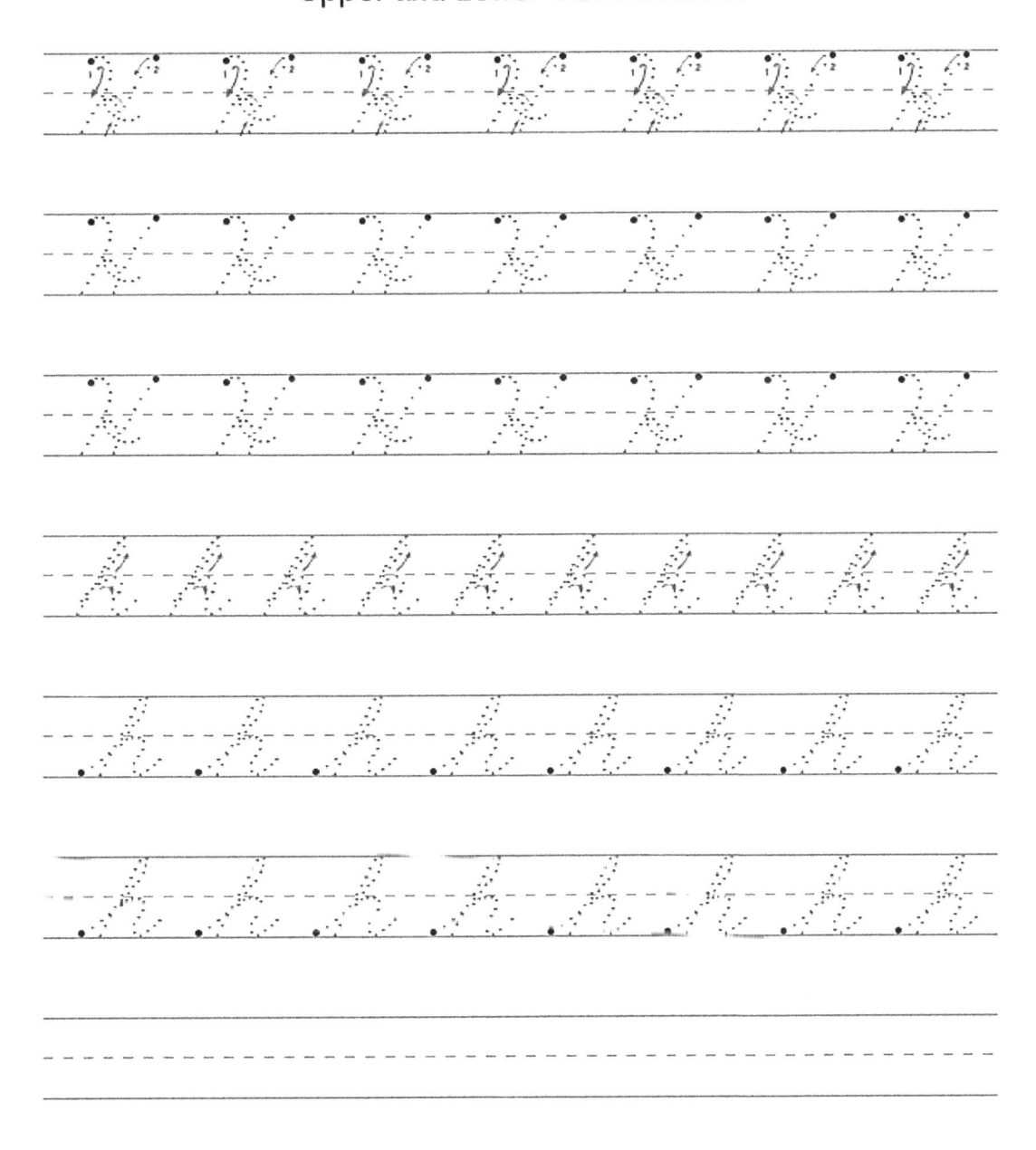

Connect the letters and write the sentences

Kathy has a hobby.

Kathy has a hobby.

Kathy has a hobby.

Upper and Lower Case Letter I

Upper and Lower Case Letter I

Connect the letters and write the sentences

Upper and Lower Case Letter J

Upper and Lower Case Letter J

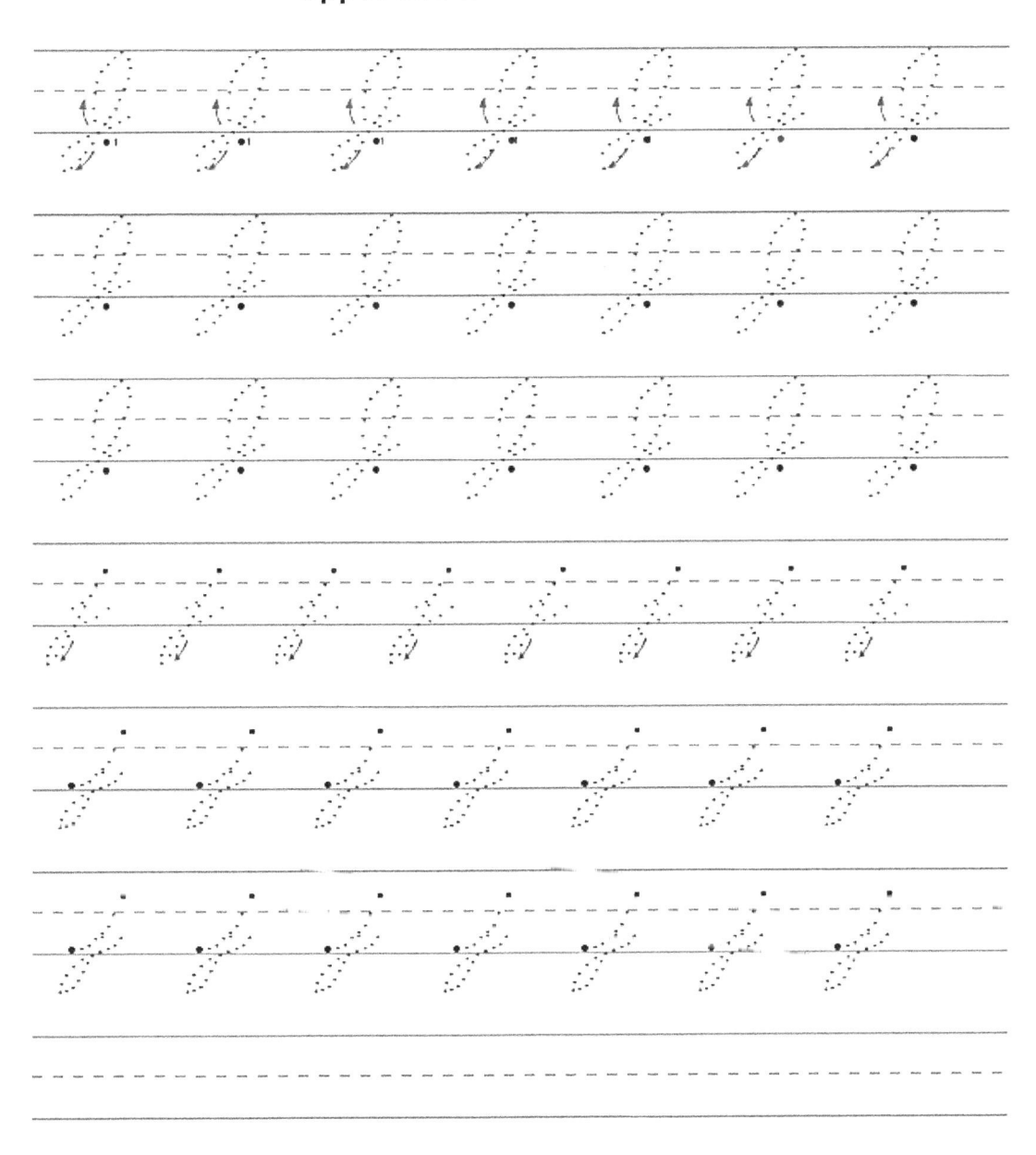

Connect the letters and write the sentences

Judah jumps for joy.

Judah jumps for joy.

Judah jumps for joy.

Upper and Lower Case Letter K

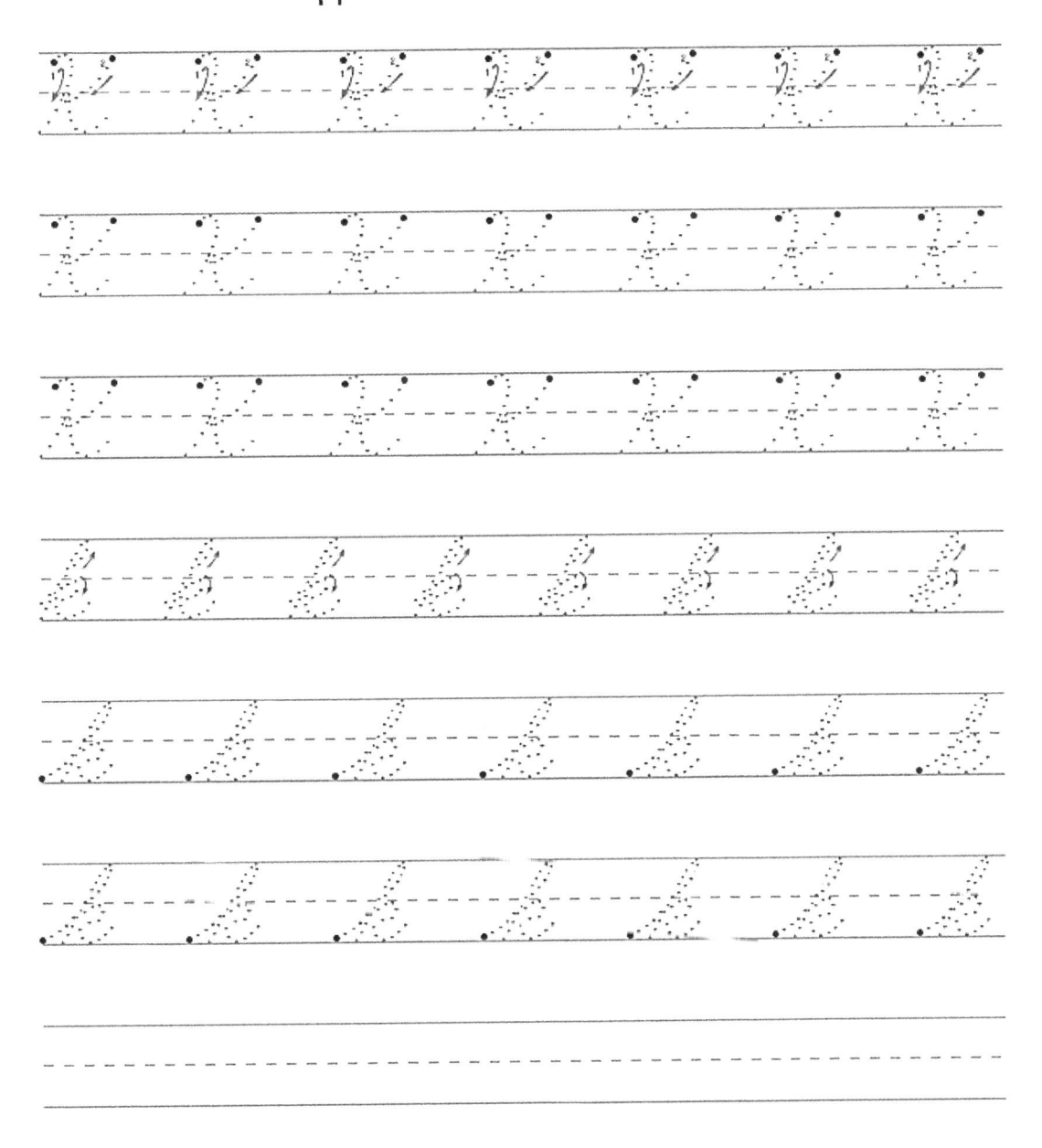

Upper and Lower Case Letter K

Connect the letters and write the sentences

Upper and Lower Case Letter L

Upper and Lower Case Letter L

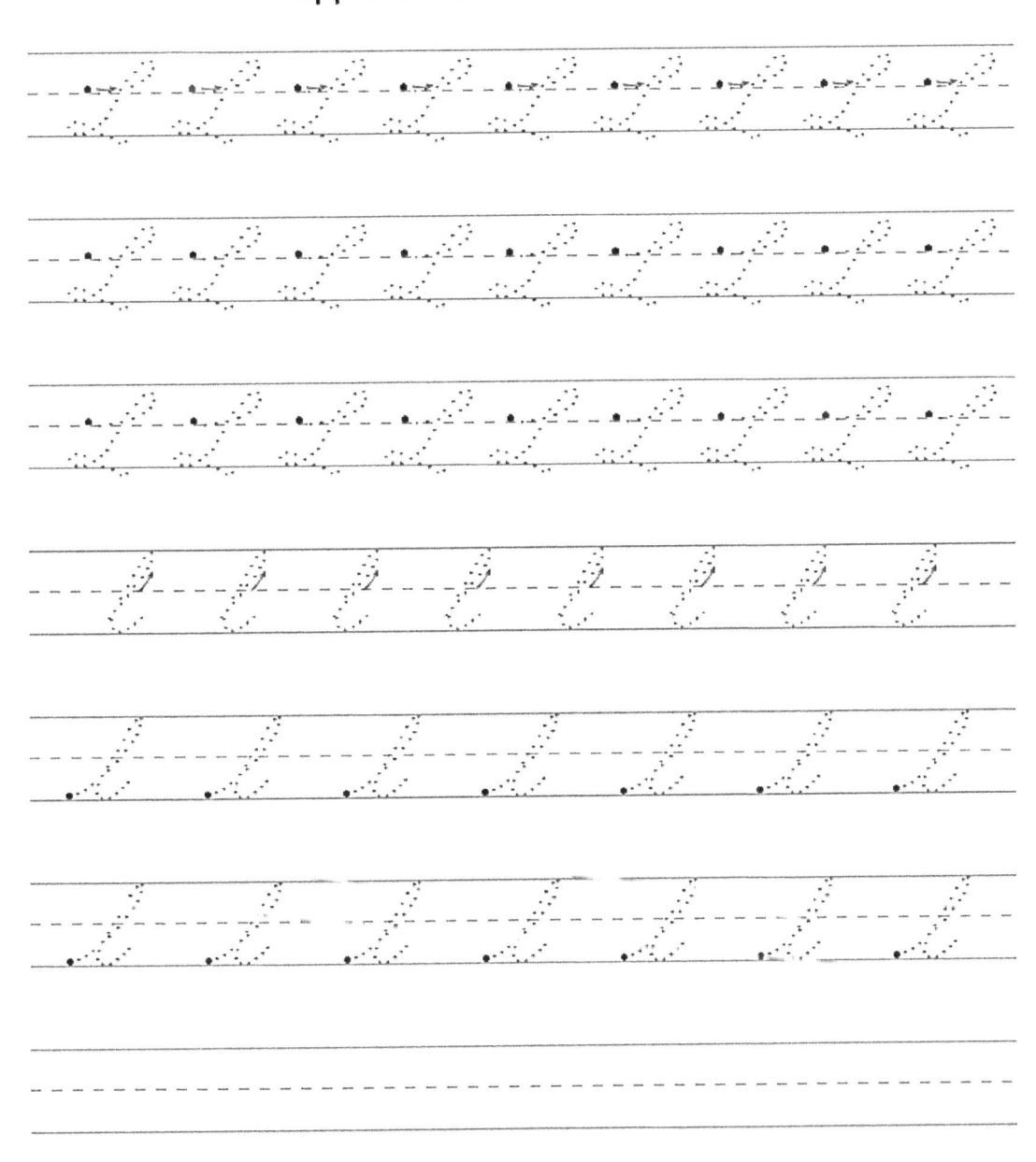

Connect the letters and write the sentences

Fanny loves Latin.

Fanny loves Latin.

Fanny loves Latin.

Upper and Lower Case Letter M

Upper and Lower Case Letter M

Connect the letters and write the sentences

Hurry makes a man.

Hurry makes a man.

Hurry makes a man.

Upper and Lower Case Letter N

Upper and Lower Case Letter N

Connect the letters and write the sentences

Upper and Lower Case Letter O

Upper and Lower Case Letter O

Connect the letters and write the sentences

She opened the door.

He found the shoe.

He found the shoe.

Upper and Lower Case Letter P

Upper and Lower Case Letter P

Connect the letters and write the sentences

Pats pats playful pigs

Pats pats playful pigs

Pats pats playful pigs

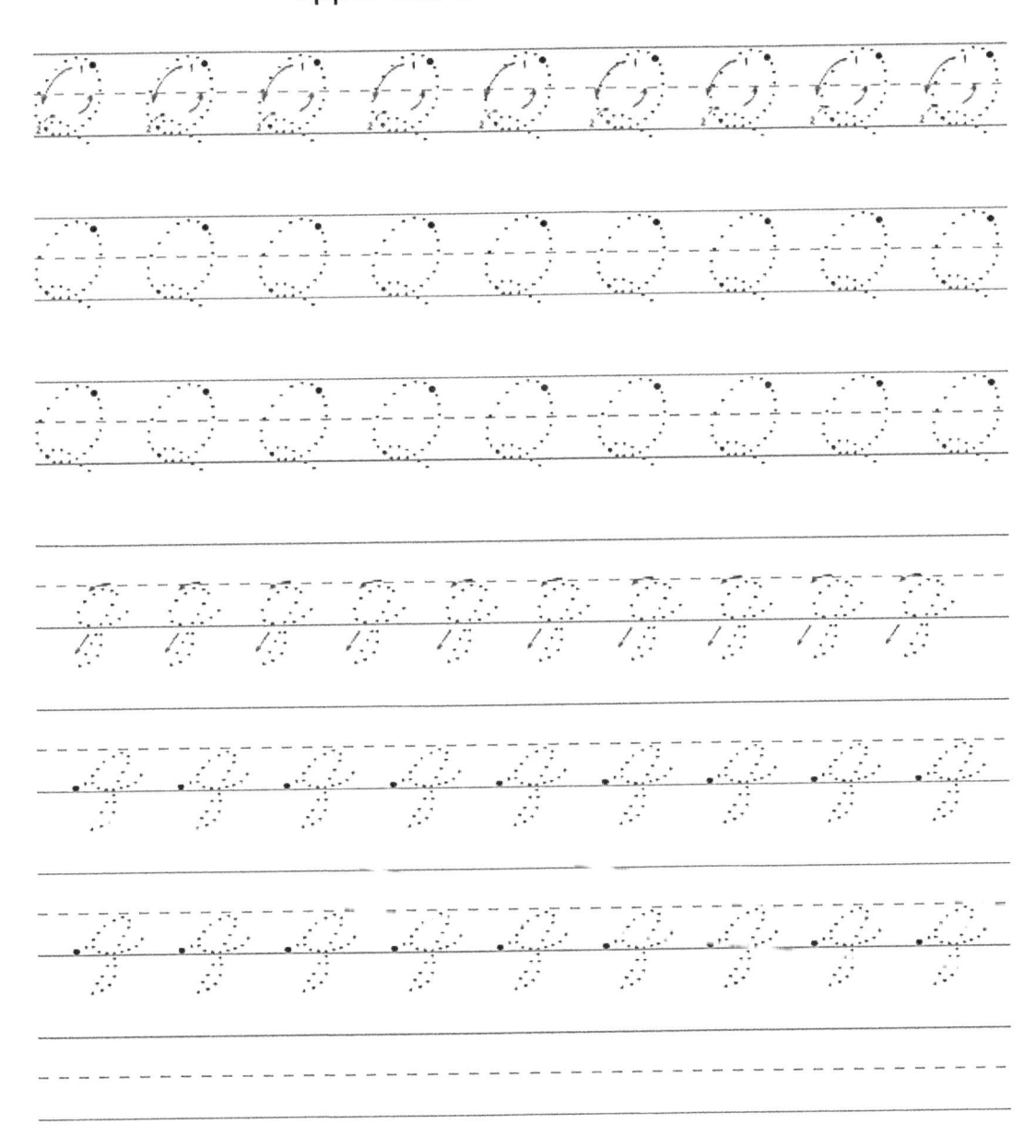

Upper and Lower Case Letter Q

Upper and Lower Case Letter Q

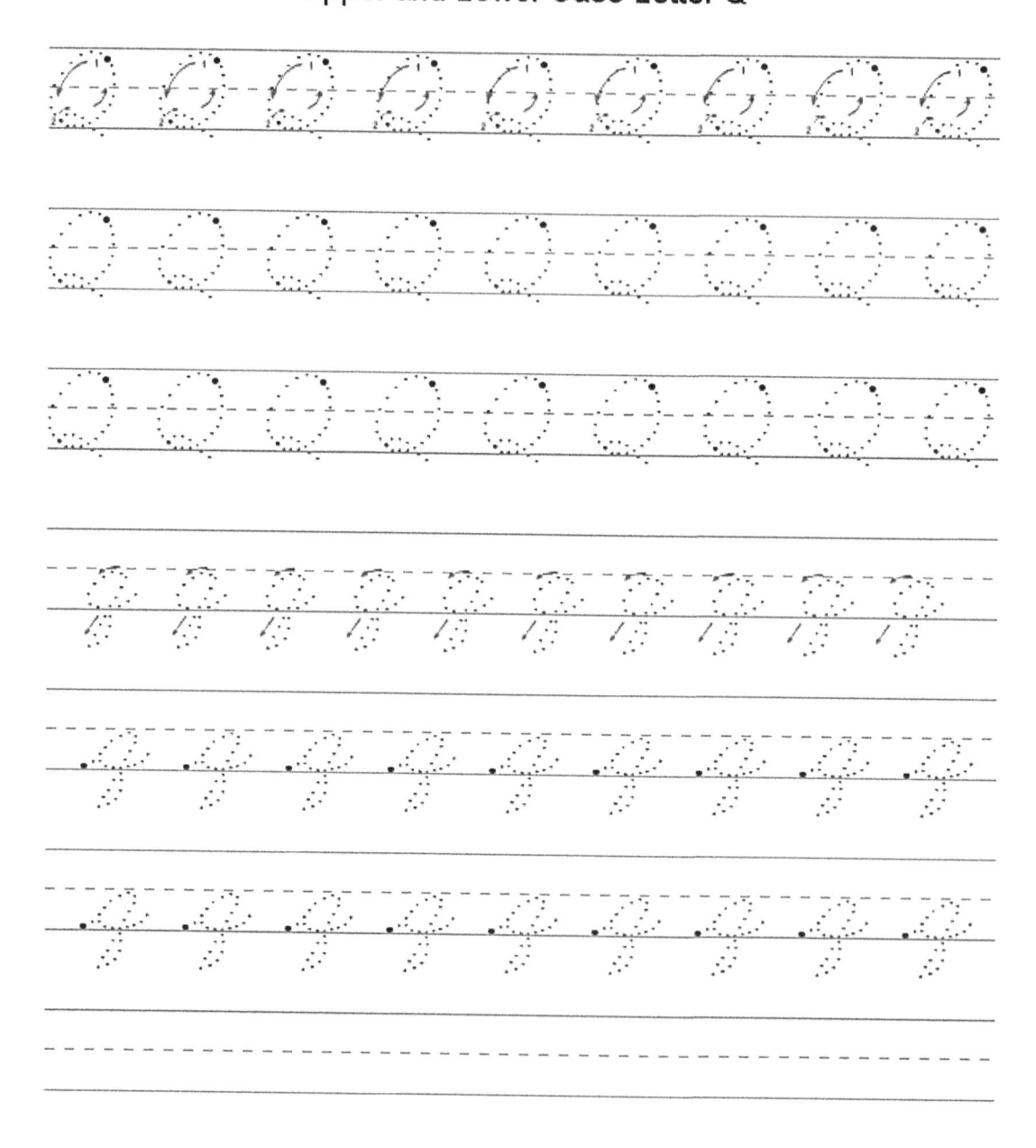

Connect the letters and write the sentences

Quinn got quidditch

Quinn got quidditch

Quinn got quidditch

Upper and Lower Case Letter R

Upper and Lower Case Letter R

Connect the letters and write the sentences

Arjun needs reports.

Arjun needs reports.

Arjun needs reports.

Upper and Lower Case Letter S

Upper and Lower Case Letter S

Connect the letters and write the sentences

Upper and Lower Case Letter T

Connect the letters and write the sentences

Tiny baby or Tigre.

Tim take a time.

Tim take a time.

Upper and Lower Case Letter U

Upper and Lower Case Letter U

Connect the letters and write the sentences

Upper and Lower Case Letter V

Upper and Lower Case Letter V

Connect the letters and write the sentences

Water travels in a

river.

Water travels in a

river.

Upper and Lower Case Letter W

Upper and Lower Case Letter W

Connect the letters and write the sentences

Wanda will walk a

mile.

Wanda will walk a

mile.

Upper and Lower Case Letter X

Upper and Lower Case Letter X

Connect the letters and write the sentences

Hamish observing an xylophone.

Xavier examining a xylophone.

Upper and Lower Case Letter Y

Upper and Lower Case Letter Y

Upper and Lower Case Letter Y

Upper and Lower Case Letter Z

Upper and Lower Case Letter Z

Jacob plays jazz at
the gig.

Jacob plays jazz at
the gig.

RESOURCES

FREE ONLINE VIDEOS AND APPS
TO TEACH CURSIVE WRITING STROKE FORMATION
(PLEASE NOTE: ALL OF THE VIDEOS AND APPS LISTED BELOW ARE FREE AND AVAILABLE AS OF THE DATE OF THIS PUBLICATION)

YouTube Videos

Cursive Writing Wizard – All uppercase and Lowercase Letters and Numbers - ZB Style Font Cursive
By APPS for KIDS
http://bit.ly/2FV19Xu

How to Write in Cursive
By Sarzaya
http://bit.ly/2FVUZGz

Write Cursive Alphabets Uppercase and Lowercase Letters
By Super Smart Kids Club
http://bit.ly/2G5TjGk

Cursive Handwriting - How to Write the Alphabet - With Instructions
By Mister Teach
http://bit.ly/2ue7ms0

How to Write in Cursive Lessons 1-33
By The HEV project
http://bit.ly/2GbrC2t

Cursive Writing APPS

Amazon - Appstore for Android
Cursive Writing Wizard Trace Letters & Words
http://amzn.to/2pwOVKu

Crazy Cursive Lite
http://amzn.to/2IJHs2P

Write ABC - Cursive Alphabets
http://amzn.to/2px827h

Cursive Alphabets
http://amzn.to/2pwWOPV

Google Play store - Android Apps on Google Play
Cursive Writing Wizard
http://bit.ly/2ptMfNO

Cursive Writing
http://bit.ly/2pwIubf

Toddler ABC Cursive Writing
http://bit.ly/2pwWUqO

ABC Kids Cursive Writing
http://bit.ly/2uewQWp

Best Kids Cursive Writing ABC
http://bit.ly/2G1ec5E

Cursive Letters Alphabets
http://bit.ly/2u8vcW6

iTunes
Cursive Writing
https://apple.co/2IJLBnp

Crazy Cursive Letters Lite
https://apple.co/2pyp6ZL

Made in the USA
Monee, IL
15 June 2021